LETTERS

TO THE

PEOPLE OF PENNSYLVANIA

ON THE

POLITICAL PRINCIPLES

OF THE

FREE SOIL PARTY.

BY JACOB LEISLER.

PHILADELPHIA:

1850.

LETTERS

TO THE

PEOPLE OF PENNSYLVANIA

ON THE

POLITICAL PRINCIPLES

OF THE

FREE SOIL PARTY.

BY JACOB LEISLER.

PHILADELPHIA:

1850.

TO THE READER

The first six of the following Letters were written for and published in the Pennsylvanian of this City in September 1848—They were re-published in October of the same year in the Plain Dealer. They had been so well received, that in February 1850, the editors of the Pennsylvanian deemed them deserving of another republication in their paper, and they accordingly appeared again in that daily, between the 19th and 22d of February 1850. On the 21st of February 1850, the author added to his former letters the seventh letter of the following series.

The present publisher, in view of the importance of these letters, and of the great interest taken in them by the public, now publishes them in pamphlet form.

Philadelphia, March 5th 1850.

Letters to the People of Pennsylvania, on the Political Principles of the Free Soil Party.

LETTER I.

Fellow Citizens: I propose to address you a few letters, in relation to the principles of the political party which has lately sprung up among us known by the name of the Free Soil party. I am impelled to the writing of these letters by purely patriotic considerations. I am not an office-holder or an office-seeker. I am only a plain citizen of Pennsylvania—born and bred within this state; and so grateful am I for the peace, liberty and prosperity I have all my life enjoyed, that I cannot be silent while I witness efforts to sap and destroy the civil blessings which I so abundantly possess.

I cannot support the principles of the Free Soil party, because they are subversive of the Union and are thus fatal to the liberty and welfare of myself and my country. I propose either to demonstrate this to you, or frankly to confess that my fears of the destructive tendencies of the principles of the Free Soil party are groundless. The fundamental principle of the Union of these States is, that each State is a sovereign and independent State, notwithstanding the confederacy into which she has entered and by which, for certain purposes of civil government, she is connected with sister States. I thus illustrate this principle. Every indictment, which is tried in the Criminal Courts of this State, concludes with an averment, that the offence set forth in it has been committed against the peace and dignity of the Commonwealth of Pennsylvania. All judicial writs issuing out of the Courts of this State are in the name of the Commonwealth of Pennsylvania. Being a Commonwealth Pennsylvania is, necessarily a sovereign and independent State; just as much so, within her territorial limits, as though she were the only Commonwealth existing on the continent. Who would part with that glorious and time-honoured name, "the Commonwealth of Pennsylvania;" and who would do otherwise than rejoice in being a Pennsylvanian?

As a member of the Union, as one of the United States of America, Pennsylvania is only *related* to her sister States. Her political existence, as a sovereign and independent tate, is in no wise affected thereby. She has entered into a perpetual compact with the other States of the Union, in the character of a sovereign and independent State, and, in that character solely, has solemnly pledged herself to observe and now does maintain the terms of that compact.

It is true that for certain purposes an Union of political interest and of political power has been instituted by that compact. A civil Government for certain purposes, termed the Government of the United States, has been created by that compact. But its name fitly expresses its character. It is a Government created and instituted by United but Sovereign and independent States or Commonwealths for certain specified and limited purposes. Those purposes are expressed in the written compact or treaty entered into by and between the sovereign aud independent States forming this Union—viz: in the Constitution of the United States. The Union, thus formed, is of its own kind. It is of the nature of a perpetual league or confederacy of sovereign and independent States. It possesses none of the attributes of inherent and essential sovereignty. It is only the creature of still subsisting and independent sovereignties. It exercises certain powers of government, it is true, but not in any absolute sense. Its governmental power is special, defined, and limited, as it were—statutory, not general. It is not derived, as is the Government of Pennsylvania, from the inherent and absolute sovereignty of the people resting on the right of the people of the State, as one of the nations of the earth, to govern themselves and for that purpose by an original law, viz: a State Constitution, to frame for themselves and, at their pleasure to alter, amend or revoke a system of government. It is simply a creature of the policy of certain sovereign and indpendent States, made by them for certain common and beneficial purposes. Its political authority is delegated, and not original. It is a Government to be known and felt by its blessings, rather than by its power among the people of the confederated sovereignties. It cannot, in any sense, be regarded as an Union, like that which constituted the former Monarchy and now constitutes the present Republic of France, viz: formed by a fusion and merger into one empire of States and Provinces, such as Guienne, Burgundy, Provence, &c. &c., once sovereign and potent States. No parallel to it can be traced in the past history of mankind. The political existence and nature of the Union is to be found only in the written league, treaty or compact which created and sustains it in being. Notwithstanding this confederation, each of the confederate States, outside of the express terms of the written compact or Constitution which creates the Union, is a foreign State, as regards the others, in all respects. Thus the Supreme Court of the United States decided, when it ruled that a bill of exchange, drawn in one State of the Union upon a drawee resident in another State and made payable in such other State, is a foreign bill of exchange.

If these views of the political relations and connections of the several sovereign States, which have framed the Constitution of the United States and formed the Union, be true, as I believe they are, the way is open to me to show, in a subsequent letter, the pernicious political errors maintained by the Free Soil party.

JACOB LEISLER.

LETTER II.

Fellow-Citizens: In my former letter, I stated the three following propositions, viz.:

1st. That the several States of this Union, at the time of its formation, were absolutely sovereign and independent.

2d. That the Government of the United States was created by a league or agreement, mutually entered into, by and between those independent and sovereign States, is possessed of no original or inherent sovereignty and exercises only limited, express and delegated powers, to be exerted with uniformity, for the benefit of those States and never to the injury of any one of them.

3d. That, by the formation of this Union or confederacy, no one of these confederated States lost or merged any part of her independent sovereignty, but maintains it entire to this day, for the purposes of observing the terms and conditions of the confederacy into which she has entered, of sustaining the delegated functions of the limited government, she, in common with her sister States, has constituted and for the purposes of local and internal republican government.

Taking these propositions for my premises, I now proceed to expose the pernicious error of the doctrine of the Free Soil party, viz.: "that the Government of the United States possesses the authority to prohibit, by Act of Congress, emigration by the citizens of the slave-holding States, with their slave property, into any of the territories of the United States."

This, I think, is a succinct and fair statement of the leading doctrine of a party, which, in 1848, nominated Martin Van Buren, of New York as its candidate for the Presidency. Let us apply the foregoing propositions to this doctrine.

But before so doing let us notice some preliminary considerations.

The territories, in respect to which it is contended that Congress have this power to legislate, are the territories purchased or annexed by the united authority and power of the independent State sovereignties exerted through the limited and delegated government constituted by them for the purposes of uniform and equal legislation upon certain subjects relating to the "common defence and the general welfare" of those sovereignties.

The citizens of half of the whole number of those confederated State sovereignties, viz.: of fifteen out of thirty States, have, it is estimated, one thousand millions of dollars' worth of their property invested in negro slaves. This kind of property is recognized and protected by their respective State laws and is their chief civil interest. It is also recognized, as an existing fact, in the league or compact into which they entered with the other fifteen States by being allowed as a basis of representation in Congress, and being protected, whenever it is necessary to invoke the sovereign authority of their sister States to reclaim it, being fugitive within any of their limits.

That portion of those territories which lies south of 36 degrees 30 minutes North latitude, is directly contiguous, on the West and South, to those slave-holding States and is between them and a wide ocean laving the shores of both the Western and Eastern world, and presenting a great highway for the commerce of all the earth. Vast tracts of fertile and unoccupied land in these contiguous territories invite the emigration of the citizens of those slave-holding sovereignties and offer a wide field for the exertion of their enterprise and industry and safe and pleasant homes for themselves and posterity.

The population of those slave-holding States, in common with their brethren of the non slave-holding States, are enterprising, crave expansion and extension of their trade, agriculture, and manufactures and seek new seats, towards the setting sun and great Western ocean, for themselves, their families and their possessions.

If the Union had never been formed and these territories were not the common property of the associated, confederated, or United States, a principle of natural and national law, recognised by all foreign jurists and by the Government of the Union in their late diplomatic discussion with the British Government respecting the Oregon Territory, teaches, that a civilized State has a right to peacefully occupy, for the purpose of settlement and cultivation, a territory partially occupied or merely roamed over by savage or semi-barbarous nations and would consequently sanction the extension of the limits of the slave-holding sovereignties over the territories which lie due West and South of them and are either partially occupied or merely roamed over by the savage or semi-barbarous Indian and Mexican races.

Furthermore, it is admitted, that Congress possesses no authority to prohibit the emigration of the people of the non-slave-holding States with all their property and possessions of every kind whatsoever, including their property in the labour of hired servants and apprentices, into these territories. The claim set up for Congress is not solely that they may organise new territories, by bestowing on them a Republican form of Government and extending to them the protection of the arms of the Union and the benefit of the National Treaties made by the United States and may regulate the sale and disposal of the unoccupied public lands in said territories by equal and uniform laws. All these things Congress certainly may and ought to do. The "Free Soil party" *do not merely deny*, that Congress have no authority, by organic or other laws, to introduce the institution of slavery into the territories of the United States. That may, with the most perfect propriety, be conceded, seeing that the people of the territories, after their respective organizations, alone possess the natural and indefeasible right of self-government and of establishing and regulating their own local institutions. *But the doctrine advanced by that party really is: "that, despite all the aforesaid political principles and under all the hereinbefore mentioned circumstances, Congress have the right to prohibit the citizens of the slave-holding States from emigrating with their slave property into the territories of the United States."*

The way is now prepared to examine this doctrine in the light of the propositions stated by me in my former letter; and I thence argue, that if Congress possess the authority claimed for them, it cannot be by virtue of any original or inherent sovereignty in the Government of the United States nor can it be derived from any other source than the express terms of the Federal compact, viz.: the Constitution of the United States.

Indeed the possession of such authority would seem to be in entire opposition to the essential sovereignties of the slave-holding States, which sovereignties exist to protect the interests of their respective citizens, to enlarge their personal rights and privileges and to increase the value of their property by encouraging their enterprise and opening new fields for the profitable employment of their energies and means, rather than to permit any impairment of those rights and privileges and any diminution of the value of that property, by a restraint of their citizens in the use and enjoyment of their possessions within the confined limits of their own States; while the new territories, the common property of the Union, are open to the emigration of the citizens of the non-slave-holding States with their property of all and every nature and kind whatsoever.

This Legislative authority in Congress, if possessed, would also be in utter opposition to the *spirit* of the Federal compact entered into by the independent State sovereignties. That spirit contemplates equal and uniform legislation by Congress, wherever permitted, beneficial to the States and *injurious to the interests of none*. If, then, such authority in Congress as is contended for by the Free Soil party is not possessed by virtue of any inherent sovereignty, is utterly opposed to the political rights and duties of the slave-holding sovereignties and is likewise inconsistent with the spirit of the Federal compact entered into by the States—where is its warrant? To this question it has been replied, that a warrant can be found for it in the letter of the Federal compact—the Constitution of the United States.

In my next I shall endeavour to furnish a conclusive refutation of this allegation.

JACOB LEISLER.

LETTER III.

Fellow Citizens: In my last letter, I undertook to furnish you with a conclusive refutation of the allegation made by the Free Soil party, "that a warrant, for the enactment by Congress of an act or acts prohibiting the emigration of the citizens of the slave-holding States with their Negro slave property, into any of the territories of the United States, can be found in the *letter* of the Constitution of the United States.

I now proceed to comply with my promise.

It might be supposed that the States, in framing the Federal compact, would make some express provision, in relation to the authority of the Government constituted by that instrument, over the territories which the Union might acquire. Accordingly we find, in the second clause of section 3d of art. 4th of the Constitution of the United States, the following express provision, viz.:

"Congress shall have the power to *dispose of* and make all needful rules and regulations respecting the territory or *other property* belonging to the United States and nothing in this Constitution shall be so constructed as to prejudice any claims of the United States, or of any particular State."

Now, this is the only *express* provision contained in the *letter* of the Constitution of the United States, in relation to the territories of the United States; and it contains not one word investing Congress with authority to prohibit emigration into the said territories by the citizens of the slave-holding States with their slave property. But does the authority given therein to Congress, "to make needful rules and regulations respecting the *territories and other property* belonging to the United States," imply the authority contended for? I answer in the negative, for the simple reason, that it is not a rule or regulation respecting said territories, as *property* of the United States, but respecting the domestic institutions of the people of the territories. Besides, it is not even an expedient, much less a needful rule or regulation respecting the *property* of the Union, inasmuch as it is at war with that primary and indispensable political duty or protection, which the slave-holding States as sovereignties owe to their respective citizens and their property, and is at variance with that spirit of the Federal compact which led to the formation of the Union, "in order to ensure domestic tranquillity, provide for the common defence and promote the general welfare," by uniform legislation, for the benefit of the confederated States and to the injury of none.

Furthermore, it is well to note, that the clause of the Constitution above referred to expressly provides "that nothing in the Constitution shall be so construed as to prejudice any claim of the United States or of any particular State.

Now, can it be said that a slave-holding State which, impelled by the same motives as a non-slave-holding State, entered into the Union for the purpose of securing and increasing the political and civil welfare of her citizens, of giving more value to their property, and greater scope to their personal enterprise and energy, has not an equitable claim to the use and occupation of the common territory of the United States, by her emigrating citizens, on terms of perfect equality with the emigrating citizens of a non-slave-holding State? If it is not denied that such a claim is rightfully possessed, then I again ask, does the citizen of a slave-holding State emigrate to a territory of the United States on terms of perfect equality with the citizen of a non-slave-holding State, when the latter may take all his property with him, of every nature and kind whatsoever, and the former may not, but is prohibited by Act of Congress from taking with him in his emigration what constitutes almost his entire means—his Negro slave property? To say to such a citizen, you may convert your slaves into money or other property not prohibited and thus emigrate, would be to mock him—"to keep the word of promise to the ear and break it to the hope;" for how greatly depreciated and almost unsaleable would slave property speedily become, if confined within the limits of the slave-holding States and for ever debarred from being used in the cultivation of the fertile vallies and plains of the South-Western territories of the Union? It is manifest that, to prohibit by Act of Congress the emigration of citizens of a slave-holding State, with their slave property, into the territories of the Union, is to prejudice the sovereignty and consequently, the natural and constitutional rights and claims of such slave-holding State. It is also expressly to disregard the first clause of sec. 2d of art. 4th of the Constitution of the United States, which provides "That the citizens of each State shall be entitled to all the privileges and immunities of citizens of the several States."

I here remark, in passing, that the question is not now respecting the social and moral evil of slavery. In regard to that there can be but one sentiment throughout the non-slave-holding States and certainly no one entertains a more sincere repugnance to it than myself. If the social and moral character of slavery is the question raised by the Free Soil party, why do they disclaim any crusade against the institution within the limits of the slavehold-holding States; and why do they not devise plans for the abolition of it in Brazil, Cuba, Porto Rico, the Barbary and Turkish States and the Russian Empire? No! the issue proposed by the party, whose doctrine is now under examination, is not, whether slavery is a social and moral evil, but it is, whether the political authority and dignity of the several States, which form this glorious and precious Union, shall rest on the basis of natural right and Federal guaranty, checking all usurpation of political power and maintaining and extending the blessings of liberty; or whether that authority and dignity shall be wholly subverted and on the ruins of State sovereignty, by a fraud upon the Federal compact, shall arise the gloomy structure of a central or consolidated Government, possessed of an inherent and absolute sovereignty, competent to charter a Bank of the United States, to enact protective tariffs, to pass into laws log-rolled internal improvement bills, appropriating the common moneys of the United States to the making of canals and railroads and other improvements of a local or sectional character within the limits of the favoured States to the entire neglect or detriment of other portions of the Union—to create monopolies, and to practice partial or class legislation of every kind, for the enrichment of the few and the impoverishment of the many.

This is the real issue formed between the true Democracy of the Union and the misnamed Free Soil party. The Democratic party are now contending, as they have ever contended, for State sovereignty and for an express delegation of authority, according to a strict construction of the Federal compact, to the Government of limited powers formed by it, wherever a question concerning the extent of that authority arises; while their opponents of all factions are now, as formerly, advocating measures, the tendencies of which are to certain anarchy or consolidation.

In my next letter, fellow-citizens, I shall endeavour to show, that however great may be the danger that the principles andmeasures of the Free Soil party will result in a consolidation of the States, the peril of a division of the Union, and of consequent civil war preceding the establishment of a consolidated monarchy or military despotism in our now free and happy land as a sure product of the political plans of that party, is much more imminent.

JACOB LEISLER.

LETTER IV.

Fellow-Citizens: Although the tendency of the doctrine, "that Congress have authority to prohibit the emigration of citizens of slave-holding States with their slave property into the territories of the United States," is directly to convert our Confederation into a consolidated Empire; yet, for the reasons which I am about to adduce, I believe, that the immediate practical result of the success of that doctrine would be the division of the Union and Civil War with all its frightful ills.

It appears to me, that should Congress ever enact that the slave property of the emigrating citizens of the slave-holding States shall not be admitted into the territories of the Union south of the latitude of 36° 30', the slave-holding States must, in vindication of their own existence and dignity as independent sovereignties, declare that the

Union is thereby dissolved and immediately establish a Southern Confederacy.

Congress never yet have taken such ground.

The Ordinance of 1787 excluding slavery from the territory ceded by Virginia North West of the river Ohio, which now constitutes the States of Ohio, Michigan, Indiana, Illinois, and Wisconsin, was never enacted in violation of State sovereignty but in accordance with it, viz.: with the terms and conditions of cession proposed and settled by the State of Virginia (then and still a slave-holding State) as the proprietor of the ceded territory. The introduction of a similar proviso of exclusion into the bill organizing the Oregon Territory caused great excitement amongst our Southern brethren; but as it practically will have no effect upon their political or social interests, seeing that the people of that territory had previously thereto decided against the institution of slavery among them, that the territory of Oregon lies North of the Missouri Compromise line of 36° 30' and that its soil and climate render the employment of Negro slave labour in that territory useless and unprofitable, that excitement has abated and our Southern brethren are not yet driven to take their ultimate and unalterable stand, in defence of their natural rights and constitutional guarantees and in protection of their one thousand millions of dollars' worth of property, by any political necessity.

When a conflict of opinion between the slave-holding and non-slave-holding States, in regard to the admission into the Union, of Missouri a slave State formed out of territory of the United States, threatened a collision fatal to the Union itself, the ardent patriotism of American Statesmen led them to agree on a NATURAL AND GEOGRAPHICAL COMPROMISE, VIZ: the line of 36° 30', North latitude. That compromise dispersed the dark and portentous clouds which hung over the Union, and has to this day been sacredly observed by Congress, to the great advantage of our beloved land, whose subsequent astonishing and unparalleled growth and prosperity are, to a great extent, its legitimate fruits. That measure, although of very doubtful constitutionality as an *Act of Congress*, yet as warranted by an *urgent political necessity*, as merely expressive of a *compromise* between the States of conflicting opinions in respect to constitutional power, was at that crisis eminently wise.

A very natural difference of opinion had arisen between the States of the Confederacy, respecting the use and enjoyment of the territory acquired by an union of their political authority and power. It was like a difference of opinion between partners, in respect to partnership property, in civil life. The non-slave-holding sovereignties objected to any extension of the institution of slavery into the territories of the Union, on the ground that it interfered with the labour and enterprise of their citizens, increased the popular representation of the slave-holding States in an undue degree in Congress, weakened the Confederacy and entailed a moral curse upon the country. The slave-holding States on the other hand insisted that it was a matter in regard to which the Government of the United States had no more right to interfere than they had to interfere with the existence of slavery within the respective sovereignties of the Union or within the dominions of any foreign power—that their citizens had as good a right, by natural law and by the guarantees and compromises of the Federal Compact, to emigrate and settle upon the common property of the States with their slave property as the citizens of the non-slave-holding States had with their property of other kinds—that to deprive them of this right would be to degrade and impoverish them and that Negro slavery neither interfered with white labour nor entailed a moral evil, where the soil and climate of a territory were unfavourable to agricultural labour by white men.

These opposing views, when mixed up with popular passion and prejudice, could not be reconciled. They could only be *compromised.* They must be compromised in some way or the only alternative must be a Dissolution of the Union. Such a result would be fatal to American freedom and disastrous to the hopes of mankind.

As when, in patriarchal times, "there was a strife between the herdmen of Abraham's cattle and the herdmen of Lot's cattle, so that they could not dwell together; and Abraham said unto Lot, let there be no strife, I pray thee, between thee and me and between my herdmen and thy herdmen; for we be brethren. Is not the whole land before thee? Separate thyself, I pray thee, from me; if thou wilt take the left hand, then I will go to the right; or if thou depart to the right, then I will go to the left;" so that difference, between the slave-holding or Southern States on the one hand and the non-slave-holding States or Northern States on the other hand, was wisely and happily adjusted by the adoption of a geographical line of separation, viz.: a line of 36° 30' North latitude across the territories; and by saying to the Southern States, let your citizens go, with their slave property, if they so please, to the territory South of that line and contiguous to the sovereignties on the West; and our citizens will depart, with their free labour and free property, into the territories North of that line and contiguous to us on the West; and there shall be perpetual peace between us, for we be brethren. Since the Act of Congress of 6th of March, 1820 admitting Missouri into the Union, the principles of the Missouri Compromise, prohibiting the extension of Negro slavery into territory North of 36° 30' of North latitude and not interfering with its extension South thereof into the territory then possessed by the United States, have been observed in good faith by the Congress of the United States. The fears of the Southern States have been, to a great degree, allayed by that Compromise, the public mind of that section of our beloved land has settled itself down upon it and regards it as a part and parcel of the American system.

In my next letter, I shall continue this branch of my subject.

JACOB LEISLER.

LETTER V.

Fellow-Citizens: The Southern States have never complained of the Missouri Compromise. They do not wish to disturb it. It is true that some of their Statesmen resisted its recognition in the recent Act of Congress organising the Oregon Territory. But that opposition may be deemed a mere feint of policy, resorted to in view of a supposed necessity, occasioned by the Wilmot Proviso and the agitation set on foot by the Abolition and Free Soil parties, evincing a determination entirely to disregard the Missouri Compromise. The Southern Statesmen only designed thereby to take that outermost defensive position, in order the better to protect their citadel. It should be remembered also, that without the distinguished aid of some of the most prominent and influential Statesmen and patriots of the South and the Constitutional approval of the President, James K. Polk—himself a Southern Statesman—the prohibition of slavery, contained in the Oregon Bill, could not have been carried through Congress. In respect to that Act of Congress the South do not appear to contemplate any further movement. But when, in reference to such portions of the territory recently acquired by the Treaty with Mexico as lie South of the latitude of 36° 30' North, the Northern States shall proceed to disregard the principles of the Missouri Compromise, cross the border line to "harry the Dame of Wardlaw's goods" and by Acts of Congress organizing those territories prohibit the emigration of the citizens of Southern States with their slave property into any part of them,—think you, my fellow-citizens, that the sovereign and independent States of the South will quietly submit? I tell you, nay. Unless the rich hot blood, which has been freely poured out and mingled with your own, on many a proud and victor-field, in three fierce wars, during the last 72 years, has lost its heat, parted with its tone, and now pulsates through craven hearts, your brethren of the South will not submit. They will not submit to an impairment of their natural, social, and personal rights—to a restriction of the free use and enjoyment of their property and the imposition of a stigma on their name and character by a sectional, unconstitutional, and partizan majority in Congress. THEY WILL CALL A SOUTHERN CONVENTION, declare that the Northern States have wantonly and wickedly violated the Federal compact and that, to preserve their liberty and independence from entire extinction, their dearest rights from tyrannical oppression and themselves from political bondage, they are compelled to separate from you and to organize a Southern Confederacy on the true Constitutional principles of the former Union. What then? Will you sneer at them and say, you cannot do without us, your slaves will shortly rise upon you, and exterminate you; you cannot thus dissolve the Union; you must return; you must yield and submit to whatever our Northern Congressional majorities may provide for you?

Methinks I hear the eloquent response of the indignant and united sovereignties of the South coming up, as with one voice, from their cities, villages, plains, vallies, and mountains and clothed with all the spirit-stirring power of a Patrick Henry, a Lee, a Pinckney, a Wirt, and a Preston, saying,

> "Though this dark cloud of slaves should rise,
> Yet nought shall blot our banner'd stars from Freedom's skies;"

and if otherwise, "Still give us liberty, or give us death!"

What then?

Will you invade their soil, fire their cities and villages, incite their slaves to insurrection, mow your brethren down with your cannon, trample them down with your cavalry, plunge fratricidal steel into their bosoms and make their fertile States a wilderness covered with their blanching bones? What then? Their sovereignties may be destroyed, the resistance of your might may be overcome,—but will they YIELD? Think you, that the watchful and powerful rival of your growing Republican greatness and power aristocratic England will stand an indifierent and idle spectator of this horrid and fratricidal strife and permit you to make such a final conquest? Will she not interpose and, if necessary, enter into an alliance offensive and defensive and fraught with commercial advantages to herself with the weaker party, the Southern Republic, the only producers of the cotton so essential to her trade and manufactures? Will the South, thus sustained, be so easily subdued?

But suppose you permit the Southern States to leave your Union in peace, can you then stand as you now stand? The motto of our patriotic sires was "united we stand, divided we fall." Is our political sagacity greater than theirs and does it hold their proverbial saying to be foolish and false? If so, a sad experience may correct our presumption. Could such a state of peaceful separation between the North and South long continue? Would you not still have to settle the question of the extension of negro slavery throughout the territories contiguous to the Southern States on the South and West? Could you then settle it by peaceful arrangement and compromise better than you can now? Assuredly it could not THEN be settled in any other manner than by an appeal to arms. Horrid, cruel and bloody civil war would thus surely mark at some period such a separation between the Northern and Southern States of this Union; and that separation must ensue, if Almighty God in his wrath ever permit the doctrine of the Free Soil party to control the legislation of Congress on the subject of Negro slavery. But let us farther suppose that the Northern States including our now peaceful Commonwealth have proved victorious in such a strife, when victory itself is dire defeat. We may then well pause for a moment and contemplate "the work of ruin wrought." Fifteen once flourishing, happy and prosperous States, the population of which are "bone of our bone and flesh of our flesh," will have been destroyed and subjugated by the superior arms of a Northern Confederacy. Will that ensure tranquillity, harmony, and permanency to any union still existing among the conquering States, polluted as it will have been with the blood of our brethren. Can the Government of such a Confederacy perform its functions of ensuring domestic tranquillity and providing for the common defence and general welfare, when all its moral power is destroyed, its checks and balances are removed and its principles of action wholly perverted? After the extinguishment of Negro slavery in the blood of tens of thousands of American white men, will it be found that all future causes of dissension amidst the victor States will be for ever removed? Will entire identity of interests suffice to hold those States for all future time together in a firm, enduring and brightening Union? Are the sectional interests and pursuits of the Middle, Eastern and Western States the same? Will they be entirely agreed on the subjects of a Bank of the United States, of a protective Tariff, of a distribution of the proceeds of the public lands among the several States, of internal improvements of a local and partial character within the limits of particular States at the common expense? Will corrupt, partizan, and overbearing majorities be THEN for ever banished from the halls of Congress? If so, then shall we have the promised Millenium, and all evil will have ceased. Perpetual vigilance will no longer be the eternal price of liberty! The veto power, with which by the Constitution the President of the Union as the immediate and responsible representative of the sovereign will of the whole people is invested—the veto power, that great balance wheel of governmental action and the potent Constitutional safeguard of the several States against Congressional corruption and usurpation, may then be dispensed with and will no longer furnish a theme of demagogical abuse and aristocratic inuendo. But what if the Millenium does not then come and selfish interests still intrigue, sectional jealousies still rankle and plot, striving parties still jostle and agitate, corrupt and tyrannical majorities still predominate, the veto power sleeps the slumber of death, State sovereignty is as "a tale that is told" and the rich, by the plunder and the waste of war, have grown richer and the poor poorer! Can you, my fellow-citizens, expect anything to rise upon the ruin caused by civil war and the overthrow of natural and canstitutional right, save anarchy or military despotism?

My next letter will be devoted to a suggestion of a reasonable and constitutional mode of meeting and compromising the differences between the public opinion of the Northern and Southern States respectively, growing out of the natural and constitutional rights of the citizens of the Southern States, to emigrate with their negro slave property into the territory of the Union, recently acquired by the treaty with Mexico and lying South of the line of 36.30 North latitude.

JACOB LEISLER.

LETTER VI.

Fellow-Citizens: It is not surprising, that a very general hostility to slavery and its extension, although it may be in accordance with constitutional and natural rights, should exist in the public mind of the Northern States. Negro slavery is justly regarded among us as a great social evil, a blight upon the community where it exists, at war with the principles of our republican creed and a positive hindrance in the way of human progress and civilization.

But the principle of non-interference with the natural right of all sovereign and independent communities to regulate their own affairs and to settle their own institutions, is a principle quite as true and quite as important to human peace, liberty and happiness, as the principle that negro slavery is morally and politically wrong.

An honest observance of national faith, of the obligations of our Federal Treaty and Compact and a strict adherence to the just principles on which, as a basis, the glorious fabric of the American Confederacy rests are more essential to our own freedom and welfare and to the political good of mankind, than to free every negro slave in existence. It must then at least be conceded, that, to state the case in the most favorable light for the political abolitionists, there is a clear conflict of duties and principles on the question of the extension of slavery, by the emigration of the citizens of the slaveholding States with their slave property into the territories of the United States. That mind must be strangely perverted, which will not hail with delight a reasonable mode of deliverance from the perplexity occasioned by such an apparent conflict of duties. Such a way of escape, it appears to me, is very happily presented by the intervention of a principle of natural and Democratic reason.

Let me premise, however, before I state that principle, that we might rationally look for some method of reconciling right minded views of duty seemingly in conflict. One truth is really never in conflict with another. It is only because we see the truth in partial relations and not in its absolute form, that we are sometimes embarrassed by an apparent conflict of one truth with another. Now, in the present matter, it is only necessary to elevate our minds above passion and prejudice, to be convinced, that no conflicting responsibility really exists, so far as the people of the Northern States are concerned.

The Almighty Ruler of Nations, the God of our Fathers, and our God, who has hitherto ever benignly guarded by his watchful and kind Providence our free institutions, has, with this difficulty provided a clear way of extrication, as will I trust be shortly made manifest by my argument.

Our Southern brethren do not ask that Congress shall introduce, by their authority, slavery into the territories of the United States and that we, through our representatives in

Congress, shall become criminally accessory to the extension of an institution which our consciences abhor. Neither do they rebel against—although they deny its constitutionality—an exercise of power by Congress to prohibit the extension of slavery to the territories North of the line of the Missouri compromise, where its paralizing influence would be felt by Northern enterprise, industry and labor. They only require that Congress should *forbear* to act in reference to their slave property, on the sufficient ground of justification that the matter is placed out of their jurisdiction by the principles of natural sovereignty and of constitutional law, so far as concerns the territories contiguous to their limits and south of the line of the Missouri Compromise and leave its determination to the will of the people of such territories after their respective organization. Now, in this reference of the whole subject matter to the will of the people of the Southern territories, I recognise a plain and easy solution of all the difficulties which environ, in many honest minds, the question as to the extension by emigration of slavery into any of the territories of the United States. The political platform, so far as respects this question of slavery in the territories, occupied by our Democratic brethren of the South and twice recognised and adopted by the Democracy of the whole Union, in the several National Democratic Conventions assembled at Baltimore, in the year 1844 and in the year 1848, rests upon the broad and well-tried republican foundation, that every organized political community has a natural and indefeasible right to govern itself and that therefore the people of the Southern territories, after their organization, should be left free to adopt or repudiate the institution of slavery as they may see fit.

Of the decision made by that popular will, whatever it may be, no one can justly complain and for it no one, save the free people of those territories respectively, can be held responsible.

It is a matter affecting exclusively the soil and labor of the people of those territories or nascent States. Any interference with their right to decide it for themselves not only endangers the existence of the Union and subverts many of our own cherished rules of right, but is likewise a foolish and fanatic crusade against the fundamental principle of self-government.

If, as brethren of the same blood, lineage, language and habits, we feel a deep interest in the future history of the people of the Southern territories of the Union and therefore must await their legislation on the subject of negro slavery with intense anxiety, it should be deemed a matter of deep thankfulness by us, that present appearances indicate, that the people of California and New Mexico, will never give their sanction to the existence of negro slavery amongst them.

At any rate, whatever may be the future action of the legislative bodies of those territories in regard to negro slavery, having left its determination where natural law places it, the people of the United States, conscious that they have found out the right way, "may go ahead" in the path of national prosperity, unembarrassed and unencumbered by the question of negro slavery. Before I close this letter, fellow-citizens of Pennsylvania, permit me to say, that you are as deeply interested in an indignant repudiation of the doctrine of the mis-named Free Soil party, as the people of any or all of the Southern States can be. It aims as fatal a blow at your avowed and cherished Democracy as it does at the property and political rights of your Southern brothers. The motto on the national shield is "E Pluribus Unum," "Of many one." The motto indicates most beautifully the identity of political sentiment and interest which ought to pervade and animate the whole Union, and warns us that a political principle, hurtful to any member of that Union, must be equally pernicious to every other member. No State of the Union certainly can have a deeper and more abiding interest in preserving inviolate its sovereignty and in checking any tendency towards centralization and consolidation, which may show itself in the workings of the machine of the General Government, than the old Keystone of Democracy—the State which venerates the memory and principles of Franklin, McKean, Mifflin, Dallas, Simon Snyder and Francis R. Shunk. Let us then set our faces and hearts, as the face and heart of one man, against the traitorous and aristocratic doctrines of modern abolitionism and revengeful Van Burenism. Let us repudiate the Wilmot Proviso and all other provisoes which restrict or impair natural and constitutional right. Let us guard most vigilantly and sacredly the Star Spangled Banner of our Republic, bear it proudly aloft, with every bright light in its galaxy unimpaired and hail with patriotic fervor the dawning of every new star on its radiant field. Thus sustained,

> "Our flag shall ever flout the sky,
> The highest under heaven."

JACOB LEISTER.

LETTER VII.

Fellow-Citizens: Since I addressed to you, in September, 1848, the six letters which have just been republished, "the coming events, which then cast their shadows before," have commenced their action. A Convention, for the purpose of considering the expediency of forming a separate confederacy of the slaveholding States of our Union, has been recently called to meet at Nashville, in the month of June next.

Virginia, the Old Dominion and mother of several of the commonwealths of our Union, has, by an act of her Legislature, lately sanctioned that Convention, in the event of the adoption of the Wilmot Proviso or of any similar measure of aggression by Congress. The Legislatures of at least four more of the Southern States have preceded her in a like authorization. All the slaveholding States are in a ferment and are with difficulty restrained by the moderate statesmen among them from at once favoring a severance of the Union.

This state of things has been entirely brought about by the reckless agitations of the Free Soil and Abolition parties, which have for a long time past irritated our Southern brethren and led them to estimate the value of the Union, in view of the injuries meditated by these parties to the independence and sovereignty of their respective States, and to their great interest—their slave property.

So long as the Veto power was in the hands of a Democratic President pledged to use it, when required in defence of their rights, the slaveholding States felt secure against any injury from the Abolition and Free Soil agitation, even if that agitation should succeed in so far influencing the opinions of the people of the non-slaveholding States, as to command sectional majorities in Congress in favor of unconstitutional and oppressive measures. But since the exercise of that power has been rendered doubtful, if not wholly repudiated, by the election of General Taylor to the Presidency of the United States and the equality of votes between the slaveholding and non-slaveholding States in the Senate is about to be destroyed by the admission of California and other nascent States, our Southern brethren are apprehensive lest they should be, at no very distant day, at the mercy of Congressional majorities, influenced by the sectional prejudices engendered by the Abolition and Free Soil doctrines. Such considerations have undoubtedly had great weight in determining the present action of the slaveholding States. But whatever may have led to it, the fact is undeniable that the Union of the States is now in *jeopardy*.

If so, what is our duty, fellow-citizens? It is a very obvious duty. It is to come up as with the face and heart of one man to the rescue of the glorious and priceless Union. It is to resolve, with patriotic unanimity, that the Union can and shall be preserved upon the fundamental and conservative principle of the Union, viz.: *the Independent*

Sovereignty of the respective States which compose it, in connecton with its Perpetual Necessity. Simply to recognise and act upon that fundamental principle, which is also the cardinal doctrine of your old Democratic faith, is all that is required of you to save the Union from the peril which threatens it. This great idea or principle, viz.: "the independent sovereignty of each of the commonwealths which form the Union, in connection with the perpetual necessity of that Union," is not only clearly expressed in that part of its Constitution, which declares, that "the powers not *delegated* to the United States by the Constitution nor prohibited by it to the States are *reserved* to the States respectively," but is also breathed throughout that instrument and is essential to the preservation of the Union formed by it. A constant recognition, by Congress in all its acts and by the Legislatures of the respective States in all their legislation, of this conservative principle will always insure a due observance of the rights of each State, a proper respect for its dignity and a sacred regard for its welfare. Such a recognition must likewise always insure the continuance of the Union, inasmuch as it makes the Union the chief interest and therefore the perpetual necessity of each State which forms it.

If this principle is always kept in mind, it will matter not how large the family of Independent Sovereignties in perpetual league and covenant may become. This fundamental and conservative principle will as effectually "establish justice, ensure domestic tranquillity, provide for the common defence, promote the general welfare, and secure the blessings of liberty" while the world lasts, among fifty associated commonwealths covering the whole continent of North America, as it was intended to do and has heretofore done among the original thirteen and the present thirty sister States.

In its applicability to our growing Union, this principle resembles the magic tent of the Arabian tale, which, while it might be carried in the hand of its possessor, was capable of an expansion sufficient to shelter the army of an Eastern Sultan.

Surely heaven-inspired must have been that wisdom of the sages of the Revolution, which laid down a principle so mighty in its power to preserve the Union in this its hour of peril and in all future time.

Proceed then, *at once*, fellow-citizens, confidently and energetically to use the talisman of might bequeathed by the wisdom of your fathers to yourselves and your posterity.

Remember that "vigilance is the eternal price of liberty", and be equal to this great emergency. Give, throughout the length and breadth of the Commonwealth, from North to

South, from East to West, in every hamlet and village, as well as in every town and city of the State, distinct expression to your unalterable resolve to apply this all sufficient principle to the adjustment of the present difficulties of the Union. Assemble in primary meetings, in all the authority and majesty of your State sovereignty and calmly declare to our excited brethren of the South and to an anxious world, that, upon the principles of the Union, the Keystone is still in her place and the arch cannot be moved.

Instruct your representatives in the General Assembly of the State, now in session, speedily to *expunge* from your statute books the Act of Assembly enacted in 1847, in violation of that article of the Constitution of the United States which pledged the faith of Pennsylvania to her sister States, "that no person held to service or labor in one State, under the laws thereof, escaping into another, shall, in consequence of any law or regulation therein, be discharged from such service or labor, but *snall be delivered upon claim* of the party to whom such service or labor may be due."

Instruct your Senators and Representatives in Congress to vote against that pestilent political heresy, the Wilmot Proviso, or any similar provision subversive of popular and State rights and to be earnest in their endeavors to enact an Act of Congress providing for the enforcement of the aforementioned guaranty of the Constitution of the Union in relation to fugitive slaves.

Instruct also the same Senators and Representatives to vote for resolutions in Congress, declaring that it is against the *spirit* of the Federal compact to abolish, by Act of Congress, slavery in the District of Columbia, without the consent of the States which ceded it for the use of the United States, or to prohibit the sale of negro slaves by the citizens of one State to the citizens of another State, whenever the law of the State where the slave is sold sanctions such sale, or to prohibit the emigration of the citizens of slave holding States, with their slave property, into any territory belonging to the Union. All of these things being speedily done, the apprehensions of your brethren of the South, in regard to future invasions of their rights by Congressional usurpation will be at once removed, the dark waves rising in the South and threatening to engulph the Union will soon subside, the clouded sky will be again clear and the stars of the Union will shine again above the placid Ocean of its prosperity with growing lustre, until they hide themselves in the light of the pure and perfect day of the world's civilization and regeneration.

JACOB LEISLER.

www.ingramcontent.com/pod-product-compliance
Lightning Source LLC
LaVergne TN
LVHW011138110826
845150LV00008B/2398